Melting Moments of Molten Lava Cakes

Satisfy Your Sweet Cravings with Irresistible Lava Cake Recipes

Contents

Introduction 4
    CLASSIC MOLTEN LAVA CAKE 7
    DARK CHOCOLATE LAVA CAKE 10
    WHITE CHOCOLATE LAVA CAKE 13
    NUTELLA LAVA CAKE 16
    RASPBERRY LAVA CAKE 19
    SALTED CARAMEL LAVA CAKE 22
    MINT CHOCOLATE LAVA CAKE 25
    PEANUT BUTTER LAVA CAKE 28
    LEMON LAVA CAKE 31
    COFFEE LAVA CAKE 34
    VANILLA BEAN LAVA CAKE 37
    ORANGE CHOCOLATE LAVA CAKE 40
    COCONUT LAVA CAKE 43
    ALMOND LAVA CAKE 46
    CHERRY CHOCOLATE LAVA CAKE 49
    LAVENDER HONEY LAVA CAKE 52
    ROSEWATER RASPBERRY LAVA CAKE 55
    LAVENDER LAVA CAKE 58
    PISTACHIO PRALINE LAVA CAKE 61
    MAPLE PECAN LAVA CAKE 64
    BLUEBERRY LEMON LAVA CAKE 67
    CARDAMOM CHAI LAVA CAKE 70
    CINNAMON APPLE LAVA CAKE 73
    LAVENDER ORANGE LAVA CAKE 76
    MATCHA GREEN TEA LAVA CAKE 79

BLACKBERRY LAVENDER LAVA CAKE 82
SPICED FIG LAVA CAKE 85
COCONUT PINEAPPLE LAVA CAKE 88
CHOCOLATE CHILI LAVA CAKE 91
SALTED CARAMEL MACADAMIA LAVA CAKE 94
BLACK FOREST LAVA CAKE 97
Conclusion 100

Introduction

Do you ever find yourself yearning for that ideal dessert—the one that delights your taste buds with each bite and astounds you with its oozing, delicious center? Are you an experienced baker trying to improve your abilities, or are you captivated by the enchantment of molten lava cakes but unsure of where to start? You've come to the correct place if you're looking for tips on creating desserts that are nothing short of exceptional.

Through this culinary adventure, you will discover how to make amazing molten lava cakes that will make you and your visitors absolutely happy. As you master the trade of making these decadent sweets, you'll encounter a universe of tastes and textures. When you:

- Learn the fundamental methods for consistently baking beautiful lava cakes.
- Discover a wide range of mouthwatering tastes, including traditional dark chocolate and unusual mashups like lavender honey and coconut lemongrass.
- Improve your dessert game with useful, step-by-step directions and advice that guarantees success with each taste.
- Make an impression on your loved ones and create special occasions with show-stopping sweets.

I developed this book as a result of my intense passion for the culinary arts and the unbridled thrill of producing something that not only delights the senses but unites others. The voyage of experimentation, numerous hours spent in the kitchen, and the desire to spread the wonder of molten lava cakes around the world are the inspiration for these recipes.

I Want You to Come Along as I Explore the World of Molten Lava Cakes. We will discover the techniques, appreciate the tastes, and perfect the art of making these delectable sweets together, leaving a lasting effect on your culinary abilities. Let's start off on this delightful excursion.

CLASSIC MOLTEN LAVA CAKE

Experience the timeless elegance of a rich, gooey chocolate lava cake with a molten center, a dessert that never goes out of style.

Servings: 4

Total Time: 25 minutes

INGREDIENTS:

- 4 ounces high-quality semi-sweet chocolate

- 1/2 cup (1 stick) of unsalted butter, cut into small pieces
- 1 cup of powdered sugar
- 2 large eggs
- 2 egg yolks
- 1 teaspoon of pure vanilla extract
- 1/4 cup of all-purpose flour
- A pinch of salt

INSTRUCTIONS:

1. Begin by preheating your oven to 425°F (220°C). Gras and lightly dust four small oven-safe dishes with flour to ensure the cakes easily release.
2. Place the high-quality semi-sweet chocolate and unsalted butter pieces into a microwave-friendly container.
3. Heat them in 30-second intervals, gently stirring each time, until they have melted together to form a velvety, smooth mixture.
4. Incorporate the powdered sugar into the melted chocolate and butter mixture until thoroughly combined.

5. In a separate container, whisk together the large eggs, egg yolks, and pure vanilla extract until the mixture becomes airy and slightly frothy.
6. Slowly and gently fold the egg mixture into the melted chocolate and sugar blend until you achieve a uniformly mixed batter.
7. Sift the all-purpose flour over the batter and add a pinch of salt. Carefully fold until the dry ingredients are fully incorporated without overmixing.
8. Evenly distribute the batter among the prepared small oven-safe dishes.
9. Place the filled small oven-safe dishes on a baking sheet and slide them into the preheated oven. Bake for approximately 12-14 minutes, or until the outer edges are set while the centers remain slightly wobbly.
10. Using a knife, carefully loosen the cakes from the small oven-safe dishes, and then invert them onto individual serving plates.
11. Serve immediately, adorned with a dusting of powdered sugar or accompanied by a dollop of whipped cream or a scoop of vanilla ice cream, if desired.

DARK CHOCOLATE LAVA CAKE

Indulge in the intense, luxurious flavor of dark chocolate as it flows like a warm river from the heart of this decadent lava cake.

Servings: 4

Total Time: 25 minutes

INGREDIENTS:

- 4 ounces high-quality dark chocolate (70% cocoa or higher)
- 1/2 cup (1 stick) of unsalted butter, cut into small pieces
- 1 cup of powdered sugar
- 2 large eggs
- 2 egg yolks
- 1 teaspoon of pure vanilla extract
- 1/4 cup of all-purpose flour
- A pinch of salt

INSTRUCTIONS:

1. Begin by preheating your oven to 425°F (220°C). Grease and lightly dust four small oven-safe dishes with flour.
2. Place the high-quality dark chocolate and unsalted butter pieces in a microwave-safe dish. Heat in short intervals, stirring occasionally until melted and smooth.
3. Add the powdered sugar to the melted dark chocolate and mix until well combined.

4. In a separate container, whisk together the large eggs, egg yolks, and pure vanilla extract until it's well combined.
5. Gently fold the egg mixture into the melted chocolate mixture until the batter is uniform.
6. Sift the all-purpose flour over the batter and add a pinch of salt. Carefully combine without overmixing.
7. Distribute the batter evenly among the prepared small oven-safe dishes.
8. Place the small oven-safe dishes on a baking sheet and bake for about 12-14 minutes, or until the edges are set but the centers are slightly wobbly.
9. Loosen the cakes with a knife, and then invert them onto serving plates.
10. Serve immediately, optionally garnished with powdered sugar, whipped cream, or vanilla ice cream.

WHITE CHOCOLATE LAVA CAKE

Experience the gentle sweetness of white chocolate as it melts into a warm, creamy river from the heart of this delectable lava cake. Each bite is a journey into a world of delicate flavors.

Servings: 4

Total Time: 25 minutes

INGREDIENTS:

- 4 ounces high-quality white chocolate
- 1/2 cup (1 stick) of unsalted butter, cut into small pieces
- 1 cup of powdered sugar
- 2 large eggs
- 2 egg yolks
- 1 teaspoon of pure vanilla extract
- 1/4 cup of all-purpose flour
- A pinch of salt

INSTRUCTIONS:

1. Begin by preheating your oven to 425°F (220°C). Grease and lightly dust four small oven-safe dishes with flour.
2. Place the high-quality white chocolate and unsalted butter pieces in a microwave-safe dish. Heat in short intervals, stirring occasionally until melted and smooth.
3. Add the powdered sugar to the melted white chocolate and mix until well combined.

4. In a separate container, whisk together the large eggs, egg yolks, and pure vanilla extract until it's well combined.
5. Gently fold the egg mixture into the melted white chocolate mixture until the batter is uniform.
6. Sift the all-purpose flour over the batter and add a pinch of salt. Carefully combine without overmixing.
7. Distribute the batter evenly among the prepared small oven-safe dishes.
8. Place the small oven-safe dishes on a baking sheet and bake for about 12-14 minutes, or until the edges are set but the centers are slightly wobbly.
9. Loosen the cakes with a knife, and then invert them onto serving plates.
10. Serve immediately, optionally garnished with powdered sugar, whipped cream, or vanilla ice cream.

NUTELLA LAVA CAKE

Embrace the creamy, hazelnut goodness of Nutella as it flows from the heart of this heavenly lava cake. Every bite is like a warm hug of deliciousness.

Servings: 4

Total Time: 25 minutes

INGREDIENTS:

- 4 tablespoons of Nutella

- 4 ounces semi-sweet chocolate
- 1/2 cup (1 stick) of unsalted butter, cut into small pieces
- 1 cup of powdered sugar
- 2 large eggs
- 2 egg yolks
- 1 teaspoon of pure vanilla extract
- 1/4 cup of all-purpose flour
- A pinch of salt

INSTRUCTIONS:

1. Begin by preheating your oven to 425°F (220°C). Grease and lightly dust four small oven-safe dishes with flour.
2. Place the Nutella in a small, microwave-safe dish and heat it briefly until it becomes more fluid. Set aside.
3. Place the semi-sweet chocolate and unsalted butter pieces in a microwave-safe dish. Heat in short intervals, stirring occasionally until melted and smooth.
4. Add the powdered sugar to the melted chocolate and mix until well combined.

5. In a separate container, whisk together the large eggs, egg yolks, and pure vanilla extract until it's well combined.
6. Gently fold the egg mixture into the melted chocolate mixture until the batter is uniform.
7. Sift the all-purpose flour over the batter and add a pinch of salt. Carefully combine without overmixing.
8. Distribute half of the batter evenly among the prepared small oven-safe dishes.
9. Add a tablespoon of Nutella to the center of each ramekin, then top with the remaining batter.
10. Place the small oven-safe dishes on a baking sheet and bake for about 12-14 minutes, or until the edges are set but the centers are slightly wobbly.
11. Loosen the cakes with a knife, and then invert them onto serving plates.
12. Serve immediately, optionally garnished with a drizzle of warm Nutella, a dusting of powdered sugar, or a scoop of vanilla ice cream.

RASPBERRY LAVA CAKE

Experience the perfect union of rich chocolate and vibrant raspberry as they harmonize in this delightful lava cake. Each bite is a burst of sweet, fruity bliss.

Prep Time: 15 minutes

Servings: 4

Total Time: 30 minutes

INGREDIENTS:

- 1/2 cup fresh raspberries
- 4 ounces semi-sweet chocolate
- 1/2 cup (1 stick) of unsalted butter, cut into small pieces
- 1 cup of powdered sugar
- 2 large eggs
- 2 egg yolks
- 1 teaspoon of pure vanilla extract
- 1/4 cup of all-purpose flour
- A pinch of salt

INSTRUCTIONS:

1. Begin by preheating your oven to 425°F (220°C). Grease and lightly dust four small oven-safe dishes with flour.
2. Place the fresh raspberries in each ramekin, spreading them out evenly.
3. Place the semi-sweet chocolate and unsalted butter pieces in a microwave-safe dish. Heat in short intervals, stirring occasionally until melted and smooth.

4. Add the powdered sugar to the melted chocolate and mix until well combined.
5. In a separate container, whisk together the large eggs, egg yolks, and pure vanilla extract until it's well combined.
6. Gently fold the egg mixture into the melted chocolate mixture until the batter is uniform.
7. Sift the all-purpose flour over the batter and add a pinch of salt. Carefully combine without overmixing.
8. Distribute the batter evenly among the prepared small oven-safe dishes, covering the raspberries.
9. Place the small oven-safe dishes on a baking sheet and bake for about 12-14 minutes, or until the edges are set but the centers are slightly wobbly.
10. Loosen the cakes with a knife, and then invert them onto serving plates.
11. Serve immediately, optionally garnished with additional fresh raspberries and a dusting of powdered sugar.

SALTED CARAMEL LAVA CAKE

Indulge in a sweet and salty symphony as warm caramel flows from the core of this decadent lava cake. It's a dessert that balances flavors with perfection.

Servings: 4

Total Time: 30 minutes

INGREDIENTS:

- 4 tablespoons of caramel sauce

- 4 ounces semi-sweet chocolate
- 1/2 cup (1 stick) of unsalted butter, cut into small picas
- 1 cup of powdered sugar
- 2 large eggs
- 2 egg yolks
- 1 teaspoon of pure vanilla extract
- 1/4 cup of all-purpose flour
- A pinch of salt

INSTRUCTIONS:

1. Begin by preheating your oven to 425°F (220°C). Grasp and lightly dust four small oven-safe dishes with flour.
2. Drizzle a tablespoon of caramel sauce into each ramekin.
3. Place the semi-sweet chocolate and unsalted butter pieces in a microwave-safe dish. Heat in short intervals, stirring occasionally until melted and smooth.
4. Add the powdered sugar to the melted chocolate and mix until well combined.

5. In a separate container, whisk together the large eggs, egg yolks, and pure vanilla extract until it's well combined.
6. Gently fold the egg mixture into the melted chocolate mixture until the batter is uniform.
7. Sift the all-purpose flour over the batter and add a pinch of salt. Carefully combine without overmixing.
8. Distribute the batter evenly among the prepared small oven-safe dishes, covering the caramel sauce.
9. Place the small oven-safe dishes on a baking sheet and bake for about 12-14 minutes, or until the edges are set but the centers are slightly wobbly.
10. Loosen the cakes with a knife, and then invert them onto serving plates.
11. Serve immediately, optionally garnished with a drizzle of additional caramel sauce and a pinch of sea salt for that delightful sweet and salty contrast.

MINT CHOCOLATE LAVA CAKE

Experience the refreshing burst of mint mingling with rich chocolate as it flows from the heart of this delightful lava cake. It's a dessert that invigorates your taste buds.

Servings: 4

Total Time: 30 minutes

INGREDIENTS:

- 1/2 teaspoon peppermint extract

- 4 ounces semi-sweet chocolate
- 1/2 cup (1 stick) of unsalted butter, cut into small pieces
- 1 cup of powdered sugar
- 2 large eggs
- 2 egg yolks
- 1/4 cup of all-purpose flour
- A pinch of salt
- Green food coloring (optional)

INSTRUCTIONS:

1. Start by preheating your oven to 425°F (220°C). Grease and lightly dust four small oven-safe dishes with flour.
2. If using, add a drop or two of green food coloring to achieve the desired mint color.
3. Place the semi-sweet chocolate and unsalted butter pieces in a microwave-safe dish. Heat in short intervals, stirring occasionally until melted and smooth.
4. Add the powdered sugar to the melted chocolate and mix until well combined.

5. In a separate container, whisk together the large eggs, egg yolks, and peppermint extract until it's well combined.
6. Gently fold the egg mixture into the melted chocolate mixture until the batter is uniform.
7. Sift the all-purpose flour over the batter and add a pinch of salt. Carefully combine without overmixing.
8. Distribute the batter evenly among the prepared small oven-safe dishes.
9. Place the small oven-safe dishes on a baking sheet and bake for about 12-14 minutes, or until the edges are set but the centers are slightly wobbly.
10. Loosen the cakes with a knife, and then invert them onto serving plates.
11. Serve immediately, optionally garnished with a dusting of powdered sugar or a sprig of fresh mint.

PEANUT BUTTER LAVA CAKE

Indulge in the creamy richness of peanut butter as it oozes from the center of this heavenly lava cake. It's a dessert that combines the best of both worlds - chocolate and peanut butter.

Servings: 4

Total Time: 25 minutes

INGREDIENTS:

- 4 tablespoons creamy peanut butter
- 4 ounces semi-sweet chocolate
- 1/2 cup (1 stick) of unsalted butter, cut into small pieces
- 1 cup of powdered sugar
- 2 large eggs
- 2 egg yolks
- 1 teaspoon of pure vanilla extract
- 1/4 cup of all-purpose flour
- A pinch of salt

INSTRUCTIONS:

1. Begin by preheating your oven to 425°F (220°C). Grease and lightly dust four small oven-safe dishes with flour.
2. Place a tablespoon of creamy peanut butter in the center of each ramekin.
3. Place the semi-sweet chocolate and unsalted butter pieces in a microwave-safe dish. Heat in short intervals, stirring occasionally until melted and smooth.

4. Add the powdered sugar to the melted chocolate and mix until well combined.
5. In a separate container, whisk together the large eggs, egg yolks, and pure vanilla extract until it's well combined.
6. Gently fold the egg mixture into the melted chocolate mixture until the batter is uniform.
7. Sift the all-purpose flour over the batter and add a pinch of salt. Carefully combine without overmixing.
8. Distribute the batter evenly among the prepared small oven-safe dishes, covering the peanut butter.
9. Place the small oven-safe dishes on a baking sheet and bake for about 12-14 minutes, or until the edges are set but the centers are slightly wobbly.
10. Loosen the cakes with a knife, and then invert them onto serving plates.
11. Serve immediately, optionally garnished with a drizzle of warm peanut butter or a scoop of vanilla ice cream for a delightful peanut butter-chocolate experience.

LEMON LAVA CAKE

Delight in the zesty and refreshing tang of lemon as it bursts forth from the center of this sunny lava cake. It's a citrusy twist on a classic dessert.

Prep Time: 15 minutes

Servings: 4

Total Time: 30 minutes

INGREDIENTS:

- Zest of 2 lemons
- 2 tablespoons lemon juice
- 4 ounces white chocolate
- 1/2 cup of unsalted butter, cut into small pieces
- 1 cup of powdered sugar
- 2 large eggs
- 2 egg yolks
- 1/4 cup of all-purpose flour
- A pinch of salt
- Yellow food coloring (optional)

INSTRUCTIONS:

1. Begin by preheating your oven to 425°F (220°C). Grease and lightly dust four small oven-safe dishes with flour.
2. If using, add a drop or two of yellow food coloring to achieve a sunny hue.
3. Place the white chocolate and unsalted butter pieces in a microwave-safe dish. Heat in short intervals, stirring occasionally until melted and smooth.
4. Add the powdered sugar to the melted white chocolate and mix until well combined.

5. In a separate container, whisk together the large eggs, egg yolks, lemon zest, and lemon juice until it's well combined.
6. Gently fold the egg mixture into the melted white chocolate mixture until the batter is uniform.
7. Sift the all-purpose flour over the batter and add a pinch of salt. Carefully combine without overmixing.
8. Distribute the batter evenly among the prepared small oven-safe dishes.
9. Place the small oven-safe dishes on a baking sheet and bake for about 12-14 minutes, or until the edges are set but the centers are slightly wobbly.
10. Loosen the cakes with a knife, and then invert them onto serving plates.
11. Serve immediately, optionally garnished with a sprinkle of powdered sugar and a twist of lemon zest.

COFFEE LAVA CAKE

Awaken your senses with the bold aroma and flavor of coffee as it melds with rich chocolate in this enticing lava cake. It's a coffee lover's dream dessert.

Servings: 4

Total Time: 25 minutes

INGREDIENTS:

- 2 tablespoons instant coffee granules

- 4 ounces semi-sweet chocolate
- 1/2 cup (1 stick) of unsalted butter, cut into small pieces
- 1 cup of powdered sugar
- 2 large eggs
- 2 egg yolks
- 1/4 cup of all-purpose flour
- A pinch of salt

INSTRUCTIONS:

1. Begin by preheating your oven to 425°F (220°C). Grease and lightly dust four small oven-safe dishes with flour.
2. Dissolve the instant coffee granules in 2 tablespoons of hot water and let it cool.
3. Place the semi-sweet chocolate and unsalted butter pieces in a microwave-safe dish. Heat in short intervals, stirring occasionally until melted and smooth.
4. Add the powdered sugar to the melted chocolate and mix until well combined.
5. In a separate container, whisk together the large eggs, egg yolks, and the dissolved coffee until it's well combined.

6. Gently fold the egg mixture into the melted chocolate mixture until the batter is uniform.
7. Sift the all-purpose flour over the batter and add a pinch of salt. Carefully combine without overmixing.
8. Distribute the batter evenly among the prepared small oven-safe dishes.
9. Place the small oven-safe dishes on a baking sheet and bake for about 12-14 minutes, or until the edges are set but the centers are slightly wobbly.
10. Loosen the cakes with a knife, and then invert them onto serving plates.
11. Serve immediately, optionally garnished with a dusting of cocoa powder or a dollop of whipped cream for a delightful coffee-chocolate experience.

VANILLA BEAN LAVA CAKE

Delight in the pure and fragrant essence of vanilla beans as it oozes from the heart of this classic lava cake. It's a timeless treat with a touch of elegance.

Servings: 4

Total Time: 25 minutes

INGREDIENTS:

- 2 vanilla beans, seeds scraped (or 2 teaspoons of pure vanilla extract)
- 4 ounces white chocolate
- 1/2 cup (1 stick) of unsalted butter, cut into small pieces
- 1 cup of powdered sugar
- 2 large eggs
- 2 egg yolks
- 1/4 cup of all-purpose flour
- A pinch of salt

INSTRUCTIONS:

1. Begin by preheating your oven to 425°F (220°C). Grease and lightly dust four small oven-safe dishes with flour.
2. If using vanilla beans, scrape the seeds from the beans.
3. Place the scraped vanilla seeds, or pure vanilla extract, in a microwave-safe dish with the white chocolate and unsalted butter. Heat in short intervals, stirring occasionally until melted and smooth.

4. Add the powdered sugar to the melted white chocolate and mix until well combined.
5. In a separate container, whisk together the large eggs, egg yolks, and the scraped vanilla seeds (if not using extract) until it's well combined.
6. Gently fold the egg mixture into the melted white chocolate mixture until the batter is uniform.
7. Sift the all-purpose flour over the batter and add a pinch of salt. Carefully combine without overmixing.
8. Distribute the batter evenly among the prepared small oven-safe dishes.
9. Place the small oven-safe dishes on a baking sheet and bake for about 12-14 minutes, or until the edges are set but the centers are slightly wobbly.
10. Loosen the cakes with a knife, and then invert them onto serving plates.
11. Serve immediately, optionally garnished with a sprinkle of powdered sugar or a drizzle of vanilla bean glaze.

ORANGE CHOCOLATE LAVA CAKE

Experience the bright and zesty kick of orange zest as it pairs harmoniously with rich chocolate in this captivating lava cake. It's a citrusy twist on a decadent dessert.

Servings: 4

Total Time: 30 minutes

INGREDIENTS:

- Zest of 2 oranges

- 4 ounces semi-sweet chocolate
- 1/2 cup (1 stick) of unsalted butter, cut into small pieces
- 1 cup of powdered sugar
- 2 large eggs
- 2 egg yolks
- 1/4 cup of all-purpose flour
- A pinch of salt

INSTRUCTIONS:

1. Begin by preheating your oven to 425°F (220°C). Grease and lightly dust four small oven-safe dishes with flour.
2. Zest the oranges and set the zest aside.
3. Place the semi-sweet chocolate and unsalted butter pieces in a microwave-safe dish. Heat in short intervals, stirring occasionally until melted and smooth.
4. Add the powdered sugar to the melted chocolate and mix until well combined.
5. In a separate container, whisk together the large eggs, egg yolks, and orange zest until it's well combined.

6. Gently fold the egg mixture into the melted chocolate mixture until the batter is uniform.
7. Sift the all-purpose flour over the batter and add a pinch of salt. Carefully combine without overmixing.
8. Distribute the batter evenly among the prepared small oven-safe dishes.
9. Place the small oven-safe dishes on a baking sheet and bake for about 12-14 minutes, or until the edges are set but the centers are slightly wobbly.
10. Loosen the cakes with a knife, and then invert them onto serving plates.
11. Serve immediately, optionally garnished with a twist of orange zest and a dusting of powdered sugar.

COCONUT LAVA CAKE

Transport your taste buds to a tropical paradise with the exotic flavor of coconut as it flows from the center of this delightful lava cake. It's a vacation for your senses.

Servings: 4

Total Time: 30 minutes

INGREDIENTS:

- 1/2 cup shredded coconut

- 4 ounces white chocolate
- 1/2 cup (1 stick) of unsalted butter, cut into small pieces
- 1 cup of powdered sugar
- 2 large eggs
- 2 egg yolks
- 1/4 cup of all-purpose flour
- A pinch of salt

INSTRUCTIONS:

1. Begin by preheating your oven to 425°F (220°C). Grease and lightly dust four small oven-safe dishes with flour.
2. Spread the shredded coconut evenly in the bottom of each ramekin.
3. Place the white chocolate and unsalted butter pieces in a microwave-safe dish. Heat in short intervals, stirring occasionally until melted and smooth.
4. Add the powdered sugar to the melted white chocolate and mix until well combined.
5. In a separate container, whisk together the large eggs, egg yolks until it's well combined.
6. Gently fold the egg mixture into the melted white chocolate mixture until the batter is uniform.

7. Sift the all-purpose flour over the batter and add a pinch of salt. Carefully combine without overmixing.
8. Distribute the batter evenly among the prepared small oven-safe dishes, covering the shredded coconut.
9. Place the small oven-safe dishes on a baking sheet and bake for about 12-14 minutes, or until the edges are set but the centers are slightly wobbly.
10. Loosen the cakes with a knife, and then invert them onto serving plates.
11. Serve immediately, optionally garnished with a sprinkle of additional shredded coconut or a scoop of coconut ice cream.

ALMOND LAVA CAKE

Delight in the nutty aroma and flavor of almonds as it combines with rich chocolate in this inviting lava cake. It's a dessert that's as comforting as it is delicious.

Servings: 4

Total Time: 30 minutes

INGREDIENTS:

- 1/2 cup finely chopped almonds

- 4 ounces semi-sweet chocolate
- 1/2 cup (1 stick) of unsalted butter, cut into small pieces
- 1 cup of powdered sugar
- 2 large eggs
- 2 egg yolks
- 1/4 cup of all-purpose flour
- A pinch of salt

INSTRUCTIONS:

1. Begin by preheating your oven to 425°F (220°C). Grease and lightly dust four small oven-safe dishes with flour.
2. Sprinkle the finely chopped almonds evenly in the bottom of each ramekin.
3. Place the semi-sweet chocolate and unsalted butter pieces in a microwave-safe dish. Heat in short intervals, stirring occasionally until melted and smooth.
4. Add the powdered sugar to the melted chocolate and mix until well combined.
5. In a separate container, whisk together the large eggs, egg yolks until it's well combined.

6. Gently fold the egg mixture into the melted chocolate mixture until the batter is uniform.
7. Sift the all-purpose flour over the batter and add a pinch of salt. Carefully combine without overmixing.
8. Distribute the batter evenly among the prepared small oven-safe dishes, covering the chopped almonds.
9. Place the small oven-safe dishes on a baking sheet and bake for about 12-14 minutes, or until the edges are set but the centers are slightly wobbly.
10. Loosen the cakes with a knife, and then invert them onto serving plates.
11. Serve immediately, optionally garnished with a sprinkle of additional chopped almonds or a drizzle of almond liqueur.

CHERRY CHOCOLATE LAVA CAKE

Savor the sweet and tart combination of cherries and rich chocolate as they create a symphony of flavors in this delectable lava cake. It's a taste of pure indulgence.

Servings: 4

Total Time: 30 minutes

INGREDIENTS:

- 1/2 cup pitted and halved fresh or canned cherries

- 4 ounces dark chocolate
- 1/2 cup (1 stick) of unsalted butter, cut into small pieces
- 1 cup of powdered sugar
- 2 large eggs
- 2 egg yolks
- 1/4 cup of all-purpose flour
- A pinch of salt

INSTRUCTIONS:

1. Preheat your oven to 425°F and grease four small oven-safe dishes.
2. Place a few cherry halves at the bottom of each ramekin.
3. In a microwave-safe dish, melt the dark chocolate and unsalted butter in short intervals, stirring until smooth.
4. Add powdered sugar to the chocolate mixture and combine well.
5. In a separate bowl, whisk eggs, egg yolks until well combined.
6. Gently fold the egg mixture into the chocolate mixture until you have a smooth batter.

7. Sift the all-purpose flour over the batter and add a pinch of salt. Carefully combine without overmixing.
8. Divide the batter evenly among the small oven-safe dishes, covering the cherries.
9. Place the small oven-safe dishes on a baking sheet and bake for about 12-14 minutes, or until the edges are set but the centers are slightly wobbly.
10. Loosen the cakes with a knife, and then invert them onto serving plates.
11. Serve immediately, optionally garnished with a drizzle of chocolate sauce and a few fresh cherries.

LAVENDER HONEY LAVA CAKE

Indulge in the delicate floral notes of lavender paired with the golden sweetness of honey in this unique and delightful lava cake.

Servings: 4

Total Time: 30 minutes

INGREDIENTS:

- 1 teaspoon dried culinary lavender flowers

- 4 ounces white chocolate
- 1/2 cup (1 stick) of unsalted butter, cut into small pieces
- 1/2 cup of powdered sugar
- 2 large eggs
- 2 egg yolks
- 1/4 cup of all-purpose flour
- A pinch of salt
- 2 tablespoons honey

INSTRUCTIONS:

1. Preheat your oven to 425°F and grease four small oven-safe dishes.
2. In a small saucepan, gently heat the culinary lavender and unsalted butter until the butter is fragrant. Strain out the lavender and discard it.
3. In a microwave-safe dish, melt the white chocolate with the lavender-infused butter in short intervals, stirring until smooth.
4. Add powdered sugar to the mixture and combine well.
5. In a separate bowl, whisk eggs, egg yolks until well combined.

6. Gently fold the egg mixture into the chocolate mixture until you have a smooth batter.
7. Sift the all-purpose flour over the batter and add a pinch of salt. Carefully combine without overmixing.
8. Divide the batter evenly among the small oven-safe dishes.
9. Drizzle a tablespoon of honey over the top of each cake.
10. Place the small oven-safe dishes on a baking sheet and bake for about 12-14 minutes, or until the edges are set but the centers are slightly wobbly.
11. Loosen the cakes with a knife, and then invert them onto serving plates.
12. Serve immediately, optionally garnished with a drizzle of additional honey and a sprinkle of powdered sugar.

ROSEWATER RASPBERRY LAVA CAKE

Savor the romantic essence of rosewater, harmonizing with the delightful burst of raspberries in this fragrant and luxurious lava cake.

Servings: 4

Total Time: 30 minutes

INGREDIENTS:

- 1 tablespoon rosewater
- 1/2 cup fresh raspberries
- 4 ounces premium dark chocolate
- 1/2 cup of premium unsalted butter, cut into small pieces
- 1 cup of powdered sugar
- 2 large eggs
- 2 egg yolks
- 1/4 cup of premium all-purpose flour
- A dash of sea salt

INSTRUCTIONS:

1. Begin by preheating your oven to 425°F (220°C). Grease and lightly dust four individual cake molds.
2. Scatter the fresh raspberries evenly at the base of each mold.
3. In a premium saucepan, gently infuse the dark chocolate and premium butter until they form a silky mixture.
4. Add powdered sugar and blend to create a uniform consistency.

5. In a separate mixing bowl, softly blend large eggs, egg yolks, and the rosewater until perfectly incorporated.
6. Carefully merge the egg mixture into the chocolate mixture, forming a velvety batter.
7. Sprinkle the premium all-purpose flour into the batter, and introduce a hint of sea salt. Mix gently until a homogeneous mixture is achieved.
8. Distribute the batter evenly into the prepared molds, covering the bed of raspberries.
9. Position the molds on a baking sheet and bake for approximately 12-14 minutes, ensuring the cake's edges are set while the centers remain softly wobbly.
10. Delicately free the cakes from their molds, then present them on individual serving plates.
11. Serve immediately, optionally adorned with an edible rose petal for an elegant touch.

LAVENDER LAVA CAKE

Immerse yourself in the delightful symphony of lavender with a hint of lavender essence, creating an aromatic and exceptional lava cake experience.

Prep Time: 15 minutes

Servings: 4

Total Time: 30 minutes

INGREDIENTS:

- 1 tablespoon dried lavender buds
- 4 ounces premium white chocolate
- 1/2 cup of premium unsalted butter, meticulously cut into small pieces
- 1/2 cup of powdered sugar
- 2 large eggs
- 2 egg yolks
- 1/4 cup of premium all-purpose flour
- A dash of sea salt
- A drop of lavender essence

INSTRUCTIONS:

1. Preheat your oven to 425°F and generously butter four small cake molds.
2. Infuse the dried lavender buds with the premium unsalted butter in a saucepan to create an aromatic infusion.
3. In a microwave-safe dish, fuse the premium white chocolate and the lavender-infused butter in short intervals, diligently stirring until a velvety texture emerges.

4. Introduce powdered sugar to the blend and amalgamate it thoroughly.
5. In a separate bowl, whisk large eggs, egg yolks, and a hint of lavender essence until impeccably united.
6. Carefully integrate the egg mixture into the white chocolate blend, creating a harmonious batter.
7. Distribute the batter uniformly into the prepared molds.
8. Set the molds on a baking sheet and bake for roughly 12-14 minutes, ensuring the cakes' borders are set while the centers retain a subtle wobble.
9. Loosen the cakes from their molds, then serve them on individual plates.
10. Serve immediately, optionally garnished with a sprinkle of lavender blossoms for an enticing floral touch.

PISTACHIO PRALINE LAVA CAKE

Indulge in the nutty richness of pistachios and the sweet crunch of praline as they combine in this delightful and sophisticated lava cake.

Servings: 4

Total Time: 30 minutes

INGREDIENTS:

- 1/2 cup finely ground pistachios

- 4 ounces premium dark chocolate
- 1/2 cup of premium unsalted butter, finely cut into small pieces
- 1 cup of powdered sugar
- 2 large eggs
- 2 egg yolks
- 1/4 cup of premium all-purpose flour
- A pinch of premium sea salt

INSTRUCTIONS:

1. Start by preheating your oven to 425°F (220°C). Grease and lightly dust four small oven-safe dishes.
2. Sprinkle the finely ground pistachios evenly at the bottom of each ramekin.
3. In a premium saucepan, gently meld the dark chocolate and premium unsalted butter until they form a silky blend.
4. Add the powdered sugar and blend to create a consistent mixture.
5. In a separate mixing bowl, softly blend large eggs, egg yolks until perfectly incorporated.
6. Carefully fold the egg mixture into the chocolate mixture, forming a velvety batter.

7. Sift the premium all-purpose flour over the batter and add a pinch of premium sea salt. Mix gently until a harmonious mixture is achieved.
8. Distribute the batter evenly into the prepared small oven-safe dishes, covering the layer of pistachios.
9. Position the small oven-safe dishes on a baking sheet and bake for about 12-14 minutes, ensuring the cake's edges are set while the centers remain softly wobbly.
10. Delicately release the cakes from their molds, then present them on individual serving plates.
11. Serve immediately, optionally garnished with a drizzle of premium caramel sauce and a sprinkling of chopped pistachios for an elegant touch.

MAPLE PECAN LAVA CAKE

Relish the warm and cozy notes of maple syrup paired with the crunchy delight of pecans in this comforting and scrumptious lava cake.

Servings: 4

Total Time: 30 minutes

INGREDIENTS:

- 1/4 cup pure maple syrup

- 1/2 cup chopped pecans
- 4 ounces premium milk chocolate
- 1/2 cup of premium unsalted butter, meticulously cut into small pieces
- 1/2 cup of powdered sugar
- 2 large eggs
- 2 egg yolks
- 1/4 cup of premium all-purpose flour
- A pinch of premium sea salt

INSTRUCTIONS:

1. Preheat your oven to 425°F and generously butter four small cake molds.
2. Drizzle a bit of pure maple syrup evenly at the base of each mold, then sprinkle chopped pecans over the syrup.
3. In a microwave-safe dish, gently melt the premium milk chocolate and the premium unsalted butter in short intervals, diligently stirring until they form a smooth mixture.
4. Introduce powdered sugar to the blend and combine it thoroughly.

5. In a separate bowl, whisk large eggs, egg yolks until they are impeccably united.
6. Carefully integrate the egg mixture into the chocolate blend, creating a harmonious batter.
7. Sift the premium all-purpose flour over the batter and add a pinch of premium sea salt. Carefully combine without overmixing.
8. Distribute the batter uniformly into the prepared molds, over the pecans and syrup.
9. Set the molds on a baking sheet and bake for about 12-14 minutes, ensuring the cakes' borders are set while the centers retain a subtle wobble.
10. Loosen the cakes from their molds, then serve them on individual plates.
11. Serve immediately, optionally garnished with a drizzle of additional maple syrup and a sprinkling of whole pecans for a comforting touch.

BLUEBERRY LEMON LAVA CAKE

Embrace the delightful pairing of fresh blueberries and zesty lemon in this refreshing and tangy lava cake. It's a burst of sunshine in every bite.

Servings: 4

Total Time: 30 minutes

INGREDIENTS:

- 1/2 cup fresh blueberries

- Zest of 2 lemons
- 4 ounces premium white chocolate
- 1/2 cup of premium unsalted butter, finely cut into small pieces
- 1 cup of powdered sugar
- 2 large eggs
- 2 egg yolks
- 1/4 cup of premium all-purpose flour
- A pinch of premium sea salt

INSTRUCTIONS:

1. Begin by preheating your oven to 425°F (220°C). Grease and lightly dust four small oven-safe dishes.
2. Scatter the fresh blueberries evenly at the bottom of each ramekin.
3. Grate the zest of the lemons and set it aside.
4. In a premium saucepan, gently melt the premium white chocolate and premium unsalted butter until they form a silky mixture.
5. Add powdered sugar to the mixture and combine well.

6. In a separate mixing bowl, softly blend large eggs, egg yolks, and the lemon zest until perfectly incorporated.
7. Carefully integrate the egg mixture into the white chocolate mixture, forming a velvety batter.
8. Sift the premium all-purpose flour over the batter and add a pinch of premium sea salt. Mix gently until a homogeneous mixture is achieved.
9. Distribute the batter evenly into the prepared small oven-safe dishes, covering the blueberries.
10. Position the small oven-safe dishes on a baking sheet and bake for about 12-14 minutes, ensuring the cake's edges are set while the centers remain softly wobbly.
11. Delicately release the cakes from their molds, then present them on individual serving plates.
12. Serve immediately, optionally garnished with a sprinkle of powdered sugar and a twist of lemon zest for a fresh and tangy finish.

CARDAMOM CHAI LAVA CAKE

Experience the exotic warmth of cardamom and chai spices as they meld in this captivating and aromatic lava cake. It's a delightful fusion of flavors.

Servings: 4

Total Time: 30 minutes

INGREDIENTS:

- 1 teaspoon ground cardamom

- 1 chai tea bag (cut open to access the tea leaves)
- 4 ounces premium dark chocolate
- 1/2 cup of premium unsalted butter, meticulously cut into small pieces
- 1/2 cup of powdered sugar
- 2 large eggs
- 2 egg yolks
- 1/4 cup of premium all-purpose flour
- A pinch of premium sea salt

INSTRUCTIONS:

1. Preheat your oven to 425°F and generously butter four small cake molds.
2. In a small bowl, combine the ground cardamom and the loose tea leaves from the chai tea bag.
3. In a premium saucepan, gently melt the premium dark chocolate and the premium unsalted butter until they form a smooth blend.
4. Add powdered sugar to the mixture and blend well.
5. In a separate mixing bowl, softly blend large eggs, egg yolks, and the cardamom-chai mixture until perfectly incorporated.

6. Carefully incorporate the egg mixture into the chocolate mixture, forming a harmonious batter.
7. Sift the premium all-purpose flour over the batter and add a pinch of premium sea salt. Mix gently until a homogeneous mixture is achieved.
8. Distribute the batter uniformly into the prepared molds.
9. Set the molds on a baking sheet and bake for about 12-14 minutes, ensuring the cakes' edges are set while the centers remain softly wobbly.
10. Loosen the cakes from their molds, then serve them on individual plates.
11. Serve immediately, optionally garnished with a dusting of cardamom and a chai tea leaf for an aromatic and exotic touch.

CINNAMON APPLE LAVA CAKE

Satisfy your taste buds with the comforting combination of cinnamon and sweet apples in this heartwarming and flavorful lava cake. It's like a slice of apple pie in a dessert.

Servings: 4

Total Time: 30 minutes

INGREDIENTS:

- 1/2 cup of finely diced sweet apples

- 1 teaspoon ground cinnamon
- 4 ounces premium dark chocolate
- 1/2 cup of premium unsalted butter, finely cut into small pieces
- 1/2 cup of powdered sugar
- 2 large eggs
- 2 egg yolks
- 1/4 cup of premium all-purpose flour
- A pinch of premium sea salt

INSTRUCTIONS:

1. Start by preheating your oven to 425°F (220°C). Grease and lightly dust four small oven-safe dishes.
2. Sprinkle the finely diced sweet apples evenly at the bottom of each ramekin, and dust them with ground cinnamon.
3. In a premium saucepan, gently melt the premium dark chocolate and the premium unsalted butter until they form a smooth mixture.
4. Add powdered sugar to the mixture and blend well.
5. In a separate mixing bowl, softly blend large eggs, egg yolks until they are perfectly incorporated.

6. Carefully fold the egg mixture into the chocolate mixture, forming a harmonious batter.
7. Sift the premium all-purpose flour over the batter and add a pinch of premium sea salt. Mix gently until a uniform mixture is achieved.
8. Distribute the batter evenly into the prepared small oven-safe dishes, covering the layer of apples and cinnamon.
9. Position the small oven-safe dishes on a baking sheet and bake for about 12-14 minutes, ensuring the cake's edges are set while the centers remain softly wobbly.
10. Delicately release the cakes from their small oven-safe dishes, then present them on individual serving plates.
11. Serve immediately, optionally garnished with a dusting of cinnamon and a slice of caramelized apple for a comforting and flavorful dessert.

LAVENDER ORANGE LAVA CAKE

Experience the delightful floral notes of lavender harmoniously blended with the zesty freshness of oranges in this fragrant and vibrant lava cake.

Servings: 4

Total Time: 30 minutes

INGREDIENTS:

- 1 tablespoon dried culinary lavender buds

- Zest of 2 oranges
- 4 ounces premium white chocolate
- 1/2 cup of premium unsalted butter, finely cut into small pieces
- 1/2 cup of powdered sugar
- 2 large eggs
- 2 egg yolks
- 1/4 cup of premium all-purpose flour
- A pinch of premium sea salt
- A drop of orange extract

INSTRUCTIONS:

1. Begin by preheating your oven to 425°F (220°C). Grease and lightly dust four small cake molds.
2. In a saucepan, gently infuse the dried culinary lavender buds with the premium unsalted butter until a fragrant lavender infusion is achieved.
3. Grate the zest of two oranges and set it aside.
4. In a microwave-safe dish, combine the premium white chocolate and the lavender-infused butter in short intervals, stirring until they form a smooth mixture.
5. Add powdered sugar to the blend and blend well.

6. In a separate mixing bowl, softly blend large eggs, egg yolks, and a drop of orange extract until perfectly incorporated.
7. Carefully integrate the egg mixture into the white chocolate mixture, creating a harmonious batter.
8. Sift the premium all-purpose flour over the batter and add a pinch of premium sea salt. Mix gently until a uniform mixture is achieved.
9. Distribute the batter uniformly into the prepared molds.
10. Place the molds on a baking sheet and bake for about 12-14 minutes, ensuring the cakes' edges are set while the centers remain softly wobbly.
11. Carefully release the cakes from their molds, then serve them on individual plates.
12. Serve immediately, optionally garnished with a sprinkle of orange zest and a candied lavender blossom for a visually appealing and aromatic touch.

MATCHA GREEN TEA LAVA CAKE

Delight in the vibrant and earthy flavors of matcha green tea as it melds with the richness of chocolate in this captivating and unique lava cake.

Servings: 4

Total Time: 30 minutes

INGREDIENTS:

- 2 teaspoons matcha green tea powder

- 4 ounces premium dark chocolate
- 1/2 cup of premium unsalted butter, finely cut into small pieces
- 1/2 cup of powdered sugar
- 2 large eggs
- 2 egg yolks
- 1/4 cup of premium all-purpose flour
- A pinch of premium sea salt

INSTRUCTIONS:

1. Start by preheating your oven to 425°F (220°C). Grease and lightly dust four small oven-safe dishes.
2. In a small bowl, sift the matcha green tea powder to remove any lumps.
3. In a premium saucepan, gently melt the premium dark chocolate and the premium unsalted butter until they form a smooth mixture.
4. Add powdered sugar to the mixture and blend well.
5. In a separate mixing bowl, softly blend large eggs and egg yolks until they are perfectly incorporated.
6. Carefully integrate the egg mixture into the chocolate mixture, forming a harmonious batter.

7. Sift the premium all-purpose flour over the batter and add a pinch of premium sea salt. Mix gently until a uniform mixture is achieved.
8. Divide the batter evenly into the prepared small oven-safe dishes.
9. Place the small oven-safe dishes on a baking sheet and bake for about 12-14 minutes, ensuring the cakes' edges are set while the centers remain softly wobbly.
10. Loosen the cakes from their small oven-safe dishes, then present them on individual serving plates.
11. Serve immediately, optionally garnished with a sprinkle of matcha green tea powder and a dollop of fresh whipped cream for an enchanting and distinctive dessert.

BLACKBERRY LAVENDER LAVA CAKE

Indulge in the lush and fruity essence of blackberries, combined with the delicate aroma of lavender, in this delightful and aromatic lava cake.

Servings: 4

Total Time: 30 minutes

INGREDIENTS:

- 1/2 cup fresh blackberries
- 1 teaspoon dried culinary lavender buds
- 4 ounces premium white chocolate
- 1/2 cup of premium unsalted butter, finely cut into small pieces
- 1/2 cup of powdered sugar
- 2 large eggs
- 2 egg yolks
- 1/4 cup of premium all-purpose flour
- A pinch of premium sea salt

INSTRUCTIONS:

1. Start by preheating your oven to 425°F (220°C). Grease and lightly dust four small oven-safe dishes.
2. Scatter the fresh blackberries evenly at the bottom of each ramekin.
3. In a saucepan, gently infuse the dried culinary lavender buds with the premium unsalted butter until a fragrant lavender infusion is achieved.
4. In a microwave-safe dish, combine the premium white chocolate and the lavender-infused butter in

short intervals, stirring until they form a smooth mixture.
5. Add powdered sugar to the blend and blend well.
6. In a separate mixing bowl, softly blend large eggs, egg yolks until they are perfectly incorporated.
7. Carefully integrate the egg mixture into the white chocolate mixture, creating a harmonious batter.
8. Sift the premium all-purpose flour over the batter and add a pinch of premium sea salt. Mix gently until a uniform mixture is achieved.
9. Distribute the batter uniformly into the prepared small oven-safe dishes, covering the layer of blackberries.
10. Place the small oven-safe dishes on a baking sheet and bake for about 12-14 minutes, ensuring the cakes' edges are set while the centers remain softly wobbly.
11. Delicately release the cakes from their small oven-safe dishes, then serve them on individual plates.
12. Serve immediately, optionally garnished with a sprinkle of culinary lavender buds and a fresh blackberry for a visually appealing and aromatic touch.

SPICED FIG LAVA CAKE

Treat your senses to the warmth of spices and the sweet richness of figs in this delectable and exotic lava cake.

Servings: 4

Total Time: 30 minutes

INGREDIENTS:

- 1/2 cup finely diced dried figs
- 1/2 teaspoon ground cinnamon

- 4 ounces premium dark chocolate
- 1/2 cup of premium unsalted butter, finely cut into small pieces
- 1/2 cup of powdered sugar
- 2 large eggs
- 2 egg yolks
- 1/4 cup of premium all-purpose flour
- A pinch of premium sea salt

INSTRUCTIONS:

1. Preheat your oven to 425°F and generously butter four small cake molds.
2. Sprinkle the finely diced dried figs evenly at the bottom of each mold and dust them with ground cinnamon.
3. In a premium saucepan, gently melt the premium dark chocolate and the premium unsalted butter until they form a smooth mixture.
4. Add powdered sugar to the blend and blend well.
5. In a separate mixing bowl, softly blend large eggs, egg yolks until they are perfectly incorporated.
6. Carefully integrate the egg mixture into the chocolate mixture, forming a harmonious batter.

7. Sift the premium all-purpose flour over the batter and add a pinch of premium sea salt. Mix gently until a uniform mixture is achieved.
8. Distribute the batter uniformly into the prepared molds, over the figs and cinnamon.
9. Set the molds on a baking sheet and bake for about 12-14 minutes, ensuring the cakes' edges are set while the centers remain softly wobbly.
10. Loosen the cakes from their molds, then present them on individual plates.
11. Serve immediately, optionally garnished with a dusting of cinnamon and a slice of dried fig for an exotic and flavorful dessert.

COCONUT PINEAPPLE LAVA CAKE

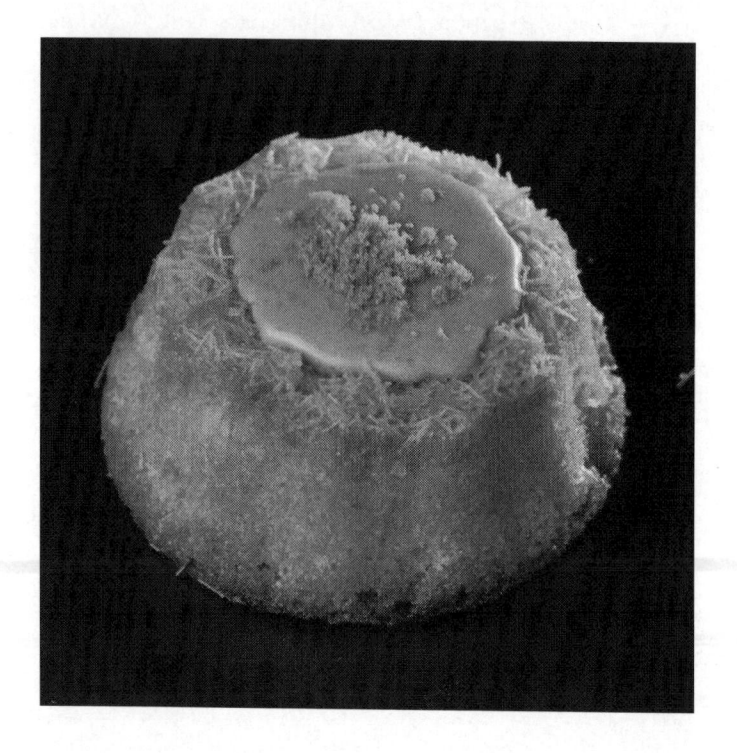

Transport yourself to a tropical paradise with the delightful blend of sweet coconut and tangy pineapple in this exotic and luscious lava cake.

Servings: 3

Total Time: 30 minutes

INGREDIENTS:

- 1/2 cup of shredded coconut

- 1/2 cup crushed pineapple, drained
- 4 ounces premium white chocolate
- 1/2 cup of premium unsalted butter, finely cut into small pieces
- 1/2 cup of powdered sugar
- 2 large eggs
- 2 egg yolks
- 1/4 cup of premium all-purpose flour
- A pinch of premium sea salt

INSTRUCTIONS:

1. Start by preheating your oven to 425°F (220°C). Grease and lightly dust four small oven-safe dishes.
2. Sprinkle the shredded coconut evenly at the bottom of each ramekin and top it with crushed pineapple.
3. In a premium saucepan, gently melt the premium white chocolate and the premium unsalted butter until they form a smooth mixture.
4. Add powdered sugar to the blend and blend well.
5. In a separate mixing bowl, softly blend large eggs and egg yolks until they are perfectly incorporated.
6. Carefully integrate the egg mixture into the white chocolate mixture, creating a harmonious batter.

7. Sift the premium all-purpose flour over the batter and add a pinch of premium sea salt. Mix gently until a uniform mixture is achieved.
8. Distribute the batter uniformly into the prepared small oven-safe dishes, covering the layer of coconut and pineapple.
9. Place the small oven-safe dishes on a baking sheet and bake for about 12-14 minutes, ensuring the cakes' edges are set while the centers remain softly wobbly.
10. Delicately release the cakes from their small oven-safe dishes, then serve them on individual plates.
11. Serve immediately, optionally garnished with a sprinkle of toasted coconut and a pineapple wedge for a tropical and refreshing dessert

CHOCOLATE CHILI LAVA CAKE

Awaken your taste buds with the intriguing combination of dark chocolate and a hint of chili heat in this bold and exhilarating lava cake.

Servings: 3

Total Time: 30 minutes

INGREDIENTS:

- 1/2 teaspoon chili powder

- 4 ounces premium dark chocolate
- 1/2 cup of premium unsalted butter, finely cut into small pieces
- 1/2 cup of powdered sugar
- 2 large eggs
- 2 egg yolks
- 1/4 cup of premium all-purpose flour
- A pinch of premium sea salt

INSTRUCTIONS:

1. Preheat your oven to 425°F and generously butter four small cake molds.
2. In a small bowl, combine the chili powder with the premium all-purpose flour, mixing it thoroughly.
3. In a premium saucepan, gently melt the premium dark chocolate and the premium unsalted butter until they form a smooth blend.
4. Add powdered sugar to the mixture and blend well.
5. In a separate mixing bowl, softly blend large eggs and egg yolks until they are perfectly incorporated.
6. Carefully incorporate the egg mixture into the chocolate mixture, forming a harmonious batter.

7. Sift the chili-infused flour over the batter and add a pinch of premium sea salt. Mix gently until a uniform mixture is achieved.
8. Distribute the batter uniformly into the prepared molds.
9. Set the molds on a baking sheet and bake for about 12-14 minutes, ensuring the cakes' edges are set while the centers remain softly wobbly.
10. Loosen the cakes from their molds, then present them on individual plates.
11. Serve immediately, optionally garnished with a dusting of cocoa powder and a chili pepper slice for a bold and exciting dessert.

SALTED CARAMEL MACADAMIA LAVA CAKE

Embrace the indulgent richness of salted caramel and the buttery crunch of macadamia nuts in this irresistible and delightful lava cake.

Servings: 4

Total Time: 30 minutes

INGREDIENTS:

- 1/2 cup of salted caramel sauce
- 1/4 cup crushed macadamia nuts
- 4 ounces premium dark chocolate
- 1/2 cup of premium unsalted butter, finely cut into small pieces
- 1/2 cup of powdered sugar
- 2 large eggs
- 2 egg yolks
- 1/4 cup of premium all-purpose flour
- A pinch of premium sea salt

INSTRUCTIONS:

1. Preheat your oven to 425°F and generously butter four small cake molds.
2. Drizzle a generous amount of salted caramel sauce evenly at the bottom of each mold and sprinkle crushed macadamia nuts over the caramel.
3. In a premium saucepan, gently melt the premium dark chocolate and the premium unsalted butter until they form a smooth blend.
4. Add powdered sugar to the mixture and blend well.

5. In a separate mixing bowl, softly blend large eggs, egg yolks until they are perfectly incorporated.
6. Carefully incorporate the egg mixture into the chocolate mixture, forming a harmonious batter.
7. Sift the premium all-purpose flour over the batter and add a pinch of premium sea salt. Mix gently until a uniform mixture is achieved.
8. Distribute the batter uniformly into the prepared molds, over the salted caramel and macadamia nuts.
9. Set the molds on a baking sheet and bake for about 12-14 minutes, ensuring the cakes' edges are set while the centers remain softly wobbly.
10. Loosen the cakes from their molds, then present them on individual plates.
11. Serve immediately, optionally garnished with an extra drizzle of salted caramel and a sprinkle of macadamia nuts for an irresistible and indulgent dessert.

BLACK FOREST LAVA CAKE

Delight in the rich and timeless flavors of the classic Black Forest cake as it surprises you with a molten chocolate center in this decadent and indulgent lava cake.

Prep Time: 20 minutes

Servings: 4

Total Time: 30 minutes

INGREDIENTS:

- 1/2 cup of dark cherries, pitted and halved
- 1 tablespoon kirsch (cherry brandy)
- 4 ounces premium dark chocolate
- 1/2 cup of premium unsalted butter, finely cut into small pieces
- 1/2 cup of powdered sugar
- 2 large eggs
- 2 egg yolks
- 1/4 cup of premium all-purpose flour
- A pinch of premium sea salt

INSTRUCTIONS:

1. Preheat your oven to 425°F and generously butter four small cake molds.
2. Place the pitted and halved dark cherries evenly at the bottom of each mold and drizzle a bit of kirsch over them.
3. In a premium saucepan, gently melt the premium dark chocolate and the premium unsalted butter until they form a smooth blend.
4. Add powdered sugar to the mixture and blend well.

5. In a separate mixing bowl, softly blend large eggs and egg yolks until they are perfectly incorporated.
6. Carefully incorporate the egg mixture into the chocolate mixture, forming a harmonious batter.
7. Sift the premium all-purpose flour over the batter and add a pinch of premium sea salt. Mix gently until a uniform mixture is achieved.
8. Distribute the batter uniformly into the prepared molds, over the cherries.
9. Set the molds on a baking sheet and bake for about 12-14 minutes, ensuring the cakes' edges are set while the centers remain softly wobbly.
10. Loosen the cakes from their molds, then present them on individual plates.
11. Serve immediately, optionally garnished with a dollop of whipped cream and a dusting of cocoa powder for a decadent and timeless dessert.

Conclusion

Let us conclude this culinary adventure with molten lava cake by asking you to consider the flavors and lovely experiences you have had. You've learned the techniques for creating these decadent desserts and become an expert at melting lava cakes with each recipe.

Your dessert repertoire has grown, and your creative side has come to the fore when it comes to unusual and exotic pairings like coconut lemongrass and lavender honey, as well as the traditional richness of dark chocolate. You've accepted the joy of indulgence, learnt the fundamental methods, and tasted new flavors.

It's your job now to spread happiness and contentment to those you care about by serving them these delicious treats. These lava cakes will not cease to amaze and enthrall, be it for a special occasion, dinner party, or just a well-earned treat for oneself.

It is our hope that this selection has satiated your palate and encouraged you to learn more about baking. This is not where the journey ends. Try different flavors, modify the recipes to suit your needs, and continue to be amazed by the enchantment of liquefied lava cakes.

We appreciate you come along on this gastronomic journey with us. I hope you have many happy baking moments and that the warmth and joy of molten lava fills your delicacies always.

Manufactured by Amazon.ca
Bolton, ON